The Drama Handbook

KS2

50+ ready-made lessons for busy teachers

Acknowledgement

A book my mum would have enjoyed

And also

Everybody who loves drama, whether they work in the field or not, can name the person who inspired their love of the form.
My inspiration was a lady called Jean Mason.
Jean taught me drama when I was 14. She was a fabulous teacher and a kind and happy person from whom I learnt huge amounts.
It was Jean who taught me most of all that the best drama teachers are those who can interest the children, stimulate them, start them off, help them on their way and then let them go.
Sadly. We lost touch and she died a few years ago so this book is most definitely dedicated to her.

Gareth Jones asserts his moral right to be regarded as the author of this book. All rights reserved.
©February 2017.

Contents

So, why buy this one?	4
Mixed starters	
The silly chair game	6
Sponny Ronny	7
Ghost	11
Fizz	12
Trusting me, trusting you	14
Air traffic control	15
30 Second Theatre	16
Light Bites	
The Balloon that bites back	18
Pick and Mix	20
Cliff hangers	22
Moving on	24
Rollercoaster	27
The Magician's Magic Box	30
Mix and Miss-match	33
Story Circles	35
Creative Constraints	36
Pantomime "plotlets"	37
Main Courses	
The Experiment of Doctor Milo	40
Time Capsule	66
The Seven Stories	69
Radio Station	72
Exploring the World of Dreams	74
Silent Movie	77
Jason and the Argonauts	80
Dessert	
Oscars	85
A few thoughts on assessment	87

So why buy this one?

As a drama teacher, or a teacher asked to teach drama, what do you need? Not a wordy essay on the value of drama or the theories underpinning good practice and not an overly complex description of worthy lesson plans, but rather a handbook with straight forward examples of actual activities that have been proven in the drama classroom which the students will enjoy and from which they will learn and develop.

This handbook contains games and projects that I have developed over the last 34 years as a drama teacher in an East Sussex Community College, and more recently as an Advanced Skills Teacher working for the School Improvement Service and as a Lead Practitioner for Transition.

It was in that last role that I taught drama extensively to Year 5 and 6 using the ideas and activities contained in this book. They can be adapted to suit any ability. Many of them promote literacy and develop social and creative skills as well as those more usually associated with drama.

The mixed starters are exactly that, motivational games and activities to get things going. The light bites are stand-alone lessons which promote skill development whilst the main courses could easily provide you with enough ideas to usefully plan for the whole of Key Stage 2.

I still get stopped now by pupils who left long ago who want to talk about the lesson when…..

It is also the case that the skills and knowledge needed for success at the highest levels of youth drama are intrinsic to the course.

And apart from that, it's a whole lot of fun, for teacher and pupils alike.

Mixed Starters
In the Games Zone

All of the games and activities in this section do have an educational purpose and these are mostly obvious. They are also great fun as many thousands of Hailsham children over the years will testify.

Many of them are adapted from traditional drama games which have developed over the decades if not centuries.

Their general purpose is to generate energy and enthusiasm and to get the children up and doing before they realise that they are feeling shy. They also develop creative thinking, bind the group together, enhance levels of trust and give the facilitator a chance to get to know the groups mood and character quickly.

The Silly Chair Game
This is a variation of a game often known as fruit salad during which the children are told to be one of three fruits who then get mixed up.
This version is a lot more fun and has additional learning built in.

Aims
To warm the group up physically and creatively
To give everyone a chance to be in the middle
To practice listening skills
To test the mood of the group and to see how much initial trust you can place in them
When appropriate, to mix the group up prior to forming groups

Resources
One chair each

Timescale
5 to 10 minutes repeated at the beginning of as many sessions as you feel is appropriate.

Method
Sit the group in a circle with one chair for each of them but not one for you. The person in the middle invents rules to get others to change seats. Whilst they are doing so he or she sits down and somebody else is left in the middle. Statements should be clear and polite and may not be repeated.
Top tips
 "Anyone who is in year 6, change seats"
"Anyone with a nose, change seats"
"Anyone who had toast for breakfast, change seats"

Discourage vague or personal comments and encourage safe and polite behaviour.

Stop when you are ready to move on.

Spontaneous Improvisation or
Sponny Ronnie, as it came to be known.
This used to be a part of the GCSE but is popular with kids of all ages. It really is the sharp edge in developing confidence and team work. Very popular with gifted performers.

Aims
To produce confident performers who will deal with any circumstance from missed queues to collapsing sets without batting an eyelid.
To promote the ability to think on their feet.
To encourage a sense of caring towards other performers.
To develop their understanding of plot and character.
To give them experience of performance under pressure whilst in a safe environment.

Resources
Various props and costumes as possible stimuli.

Timescale
20 minute sessions as starters or popular as a way to end of days work.

Method
Choose one person and allow them to choose three others {Keep groups small, each person you add makes it 10 times harder}. Put them in the performance space and explain the rules and objectives, which are:-
- No discussion at all of what is going to happen, including off stage during the activity. Everything said must be in character.
- They must be in character all the time.
- They can do nothing in front of you that they wouldn't do in front of their parents {or a suitable authority figure}. If you don't say this, somebody will.

- They must not openly reject somebody else's contribution. For example, if student A says, "How much longer do you think we'll be stuck in this dungeon"? Student B should not say, "Nice spaceship". They must work with the contribution however hard that might be.
- They can be creative but the work must be closely related to the stimulus.
- They should be aware of other members of their group and do their best to make sure that everyone has a chance to get involved.
- They should avoid taking it in turns to have their moment in the spotlight.
- They should challenge themselves to produce their best work.
- They should always be on the lookout for an effective ending.

It is vital that every performance is followed by a frank debriefing in which successes and failures are discussed in a supportive way.

Possible Stimuli
These fall in to the usual groups i.e. A title, props, costume, a piece of text
{A newspaper headline, poetry, prose, book title, quote etc.} a piece of music or a sound effect, a beginning of a situation. I've listed a number of these below but I'm sure that you will think of many more.

Titles and situations, in no particular order:

The House at the top of the Hill
On an airplane, somebody becomes seriously ill
You are waiting at a bus stop. Something happens
Shop lifting
The airport departure lounge
A letter arrives containing good news / bad news
The Lottery
The Waiting room
The unexpected meeting
The Accident

- The Argument
- A bad day at school / work
- Customs
- The Big Lie
- Ghost story
- The locked door
- The terrible holiday
- The blind date
- At the Doctors / Dentists
- The Operation
- The Party
- A strange present
- The black box
- The dream that came true
- Leaving home
- Dad found out
- The journey of no return
- I thought I'd killed him / her / it
- The reunion
- The intervention
- The black bag
- There's somebody there
- Don't look now
- Dangerous operation
- The problem with….{Name somebody in the group}
- The island of adventure
- Spy story
- He rescue
- The great Christmas disaster
- The old castle
- Arctic explorers
- Psychopath
- These four walls
- The inheritance
- Revenge
- 5 minutes to go
- The first day in the army / school / on the moon
- Alien
- The bully
- The gas leak
- The tap that won't turn off
- The haunted tent / house / shoes / etc
- Trapped
- The lift is stuck
- Blackmail
- The unexpected visitor
- Mistaken identity
- Pay up
- Day trip to France
- False alarm
- The poisoned peach
- The restaurant from hell

9

The reject
The big freeze
The hole at the pole
Problem child
My best friend is.........
The stolen........
Young offenders
Game show
Runaway

Props and music gathered to your taste.

Ghost

This one is really good for working out the group dynamics and identifying leaders. It also promotes controlled and focused working practices.

Aims
To provide an opportunity for the teacher to explore the group dynamic.
To develop skills of awareness, control and responsibility within the individual as part of the group.
To calm down groups that are having too much fun!

Resources
A clean floor in a large enough space

Timescale
5 minutes per game

Method
Get all the students to lie on the floor with their eyes closed. Touch one gently on the top of the head. That child can then get up and touch two more who each touch two more until only one child is left. Everyone gathers around that one child and on the count of three shouts "boo" in their ear.
The games only works if total silence is maintained and often fails initially either because there is too much noise or because, all of a sudden, there is no one left lying down. It is always interesting to watch leaders emerge and plans being made as they try to make it happen.
Always start the next game by choosing the person who was yelled at in the previous one and make sure that no one is yelled at twice.

Top tip
Choose obviously nervous children first and allow yourself to choose as many as you feel is right.

Fizz
This is a hot favourite. Sit the group in a circle and explain whilst demonstrating the simple rules of the game. It can be played to establish records or as an individual or team game. Games of Fizz have been known to last for hours.

Aims
This is a competitive game which does any number of things:
- It aims to develop reaction speeds and levels of concentration.
- It engenders team spirit and allows team building when played one group against another or to establish records.
- It encourages confidence and participation.
- It is a fun way to get the class warmed up and concentrating.

Resources
One chair each

Timescale
At least five minutes a game but could be much longer.

Method
The rules are as follows. You can play with all competing to win or in teams.
- The fizz is an invisible object which sits in your hand and which must be passed around the circle.
- To pass it to the left you put your right hand across your body pointing left and say fizz.
- To pass it to the right you do the opposite.
- If the fizz is approaching from the left and you want to send it back in the other direction you put up your right arm, bent at the elbow with a clenched fist and say "Boing".
- To send it back to the right you do the opposite.
- You can also send it across the circle by pointing clearly with both hands and saying "Bounce".

And that's pretty much it EXCEPT,
- You can't "Boing" a "Bounce" and
- You can't "Bounce" to the person next to you.

Any mistakes and you are out. If you are out you remain part of the circle but just turn your chair around, but note,

If player 1 is in but players 3, 4, 5, 6 etc are out, then player 7 is next to player 1 and if 7 then "Bounces" to 1, then 7 is out, and vice versa.

After the rules are learnt the game should be played as fast as possible.

As a variation, you can also play the game silently. This is courtesy of a year 6 boy called AJ who suggested it.

Trusting me, trusting you.
This is a safe and easy way of finding out what sort of group you have in front of you.

Aims
To encourage a sense of trust between the members of the group
To break down physical barriers
To allow teacher assessment of the group

Resources
A working space

Timescale
5 minutes, repeated as often as you want

Method.
First, ask for a volunteer and demonstrate. You should stand behind your volunteer and explain what is going to happen. They are going to close their eyes and fall backwards, making no attempt to protect themselves. You are going to catch them before they hit the floor.
If they trust you they will not move their feet, they will not bend at the waist, they will not move their arms from their sides and they will keep their eyes closed.
When they are completing the exercise they should take it in turns to fall.

Top tips
Make sure the catcher is close to the faller and about the same size. Make sure that they understand that the further the faller falls the harder they will be to stop and that the catcher stands in a braced position.
Make it very clear that this is not a game and that they must not let their friends fall.

Air traffic control

There is no real reason why this game is called Air traffic control, it just is. When you know groups well you can extend this one and be really adventurous.

Aims
To develop trust and a sense of responsibility.
To give some understanding of what it is like to live without sight.

Resources
A safe and suitable space

Timescale
10 minutes repeated as often as you wish

Method
The children work in pairs. One closes their eyes, or is blind folded. They hold up one hand palm down. The other places the tip of one finger against the down turned palm. That is the only communication that is allowed. The controller leads the blind airplane around the space, avoiding collisions. This should go on long enough to disorientate the person who is being led. Then they change over and repeat the exercise.

Top tips
You can extend this by sending them off around the school or college. If you do you should allow verbal instructions when they come to staircases or other hazards.

30 Second Theatre
A top favourite with the children. I often find them playing this around the school at lunchtime. This is an exciting warm up activity which leads to swift formation of groups

Aims
To promote focused discussion and decision making as well as a rapid angst free introduction to performing.
To swiftly develop an understanding of how plots are constructed and particularly the importance of a planned ending.

Resources
None

Timescale
20 minutes per go or 3 goes per session. Return occasionally.

Method
Introduce the activity as a game. Tell them that they are going to move randomly round the room and that you are going to call out a number. They must them get in to groups of exactly that number, no more no less, then sit on the floor. You will then allocate stragglers. When this is done you call out a title of your own or one from the many listed below. They will then have 30 seconds to create a play {in actual fact it is usually about 2 minutes}. Each group in turn will then perform their play followed by a short debrief.

The usual plays last about 25 seconds and consist of one good idea. ALWAYS stress the need to plan the ending. As a development you could use the same starter several times and each time ask for a different plot.

Favourite titles
If you go down to the woods today you're in for a big surprise!
Now you're for it!

I wonder what's in that box {Or behind that door}?
That wasn't there last time I looked
It's gone!
Is it meant to look like that?
What happened to ………….
It's no good, it's stuck!
I wouldn't do that if I were you.
Leave it alone!
He / she's coming!
Aaarrgh!
It came off in my hand, honest.

Top tip
You can find loads more ideas in the Sponny Ronnie section.

Light Bites

Now it's time to look at some more substantial pieces. Having said that they will fit in to 1 session or maybe 3.
They all have an individual flavour and are all tried and tested successes with children over a wide age range.

The Balloon that bites back

I first saw a man performing this routine in Bath outside the pump room in the eighties. It was so effective and had such obvious potential that I've been suing it with children ever since.

Aims
To further explore the problems of physical mime
To develop the children's understanding of how to be funny
To develop the skills involved in team work with a physical outcome

Timescale
Between 1 and 3 sessions, depending on the group.

Resources
Lots of balloons and the bigger the better, although packs of ordinary rounded balloons would be fine

Method
This one has to start with a demonstration.

Take a balloon firmly in hand using a broad grip. Pretend to walk down the road. Suddenly leave it behind as if it has become fixed in the air.
Try but fail to pull it.
Try but fail to push it.
Strain and go red as you exert yourself.
Suddenly, the balloon takes off and drags you with it.
It stops again.
You ask one of the children to help, {Choose a helpful one}.
Between you try and move it. Fail.

Let go in disgust and watch in amazement as it floats to the ground.

Tell the children to work in pairs with one balloon between two. They should now try to create their own comedy routine based on what they have seen.
Emphasise that the illusion is lost if the balloon is allowed to float. It must be controlled at all times, except at the end.

When they are ready, perform and debrief.

Top tip
You will need lots of spare balloons, and it helps if you have a balloon pump.

Pick and Mix
Or
How to construct a story

I've used this one with year 6 groups all the way through to A level. The results are obviously very different depending on the age and experience of the students, but it is always rewarding and really gets the participants thinking about how stories work and what they need in them to make them effective.

Aims
By the end of the activity the pupils should have an understanding of the need for interesting characters, events and locations in the effective telling of a tale.

Time scale
Between 1 and 3 sessions. 50 mins to 150mins, depending on the group.

Resources
Board pen and board or sugar paper.

Method
Draw three broad columns on a board or piece of sugar paper. They should be headed "Characters"
"Events"
"Location / Place"

Ask the group as a whole to suggest things that they could write in each column. Encourage them to link them. For example you might get "Pirate", "Kidnapping", "Ship" or "Ghost", "Haunting", "Castle". When you have enough ideas form groups of a suitable size and ask them to improvise a story that must use at least on example from each column. Some will be able to use many.
When they are ready perform, and discuss with the emphasis on whether the story was actually told and did it hold their interest.

Top tip
The more advanced the group the more elements you can use and the more complex you can make them.

Cliff Hangers.

In these days of soaps and mini-series this one is a particular favourite. It's useful because you can return to it time and again over the years. I've found that it works best with years 8 and 9. With older children you tend to get a satirical take on the idea.

Aims
To explore the critical elements of cliff hanger serials
To motivate the students by using stimuli with which they are familiar and often absorbed
To stretch them by setting them the task of developing their stories and characters over an extended period
To develop their understanding of the essential elements of plot
To develop an understanding of how tension is created

Resources
Whatever props and costumes may be required. This often includes obviously fake cameras and boom mikes which slip in to view.

Timescale
Two initial lessons {Episodes 1 and 2} but returned to over a period of time as appropriate.

Method
Begin by telling them about the sort of cliff hanger endings that used to be found at the end of every episode of children's Saturday morning film series, the sort of ending where the heroine is tried to the railway track as the hero comes thundering over the hill as the credits role, only to find that next week the train is suddenly half a mile away again.
They will link this to soaps that they watch.
You can also talk about stock characters, one of which appeals to or interests a particular part of the market, and the need to have more than one plot line running at a time so that everyone remains interested.

If you choose to you could talk about how the pressure of producing these series often produces errors that can't be corrected and the need for cue cards which are obviously being read.
The other essential element is the strong sense of location and this should be their first decision.

Groups should be around 6 and it's OK to have an irate Director. Once they have chosen their location they can begin to develop their characters and stories. Keep them short. Actual screen time in most soap episodes doesn't amount to much.

After a brief development time perform and debrief making sure that each piece ended with a moment of suspense.

In the second session you can do episode 2 which starts with a rerun of the end of episode 1, maybe involving some subtle change that allows the character to get out of the mess they were in.

Top tip
Discourage parodies of current soaps. These tend to be clichéd and undemanding {Not the soaps, the parodies}.

Moving On

There are very few drama teachers trained to deliver real mime. Even so we can give the children a flavour of the art and teach them a useful skill that will contribute to the quality of their performances. Mime in this unit means creating the illusion that something is real which clearly isn't. An imagined cup, a window to climb through, a car, a rollercoaster, a magic cabinet. The only limit is the imagination of the children

Aims
To introduce the children to the essential basics of simple mime
To explore the possibilities of non-verbal communication
To enable the children to use simple mime techniques in their other drama work.

Resources
None

Timescale
This can be delivered in short burst over a long period, or in one block of about 6 to 8 sessions.

Method
This is a progressive unit with each step adding in more skills. The first is the simplest of mimes and is for individuals

Step One
Sit the children on chairs in a circle. Explain that this is a homework task. You can follow my script or use your own.

Tonight, when you get home, I want you to walk in to a room where one of your parents is, say "Hi" and then react as if you have seen something amazing in the middle of the carpet {you should do this yourself as you describe it}. Circle around it keeping your gaze firmly fixed at the same spot. When you have got your parents attention, approach the spot really carefully. When you are close enough put your hands out flat and wide and bring them together to grip the invisible box. Pick it up with your elbows locked against your ribs. Keep your eyes on it and walk over to your parent. Pass it carefully to them. Most will take it off you. Some may then call a Doctor.

One parent actually took the box and put it on the side board and then, next morning, gave it back to the boy to take back to school.

Now you have a go. Pick your spot, really focus on it. Pick up your box and pass it on.

Step Two
Now imagine that the box is bigger and very heavy. How do you create the illusion of weight? You get right down low bending your knees and keeping your back straight. Then you push your flat fingers under the box and lift. Put tension into your arms to make them shake. Make your face go red and keep your legs bent as you stagger forward a few paces before you drop it. Mop your brow and pretend to be out of breath. Now have a go. When you've practiced some of you may want to show your work

Step Three
Ask a friend to help you. Make sure the box is the same size for both of you and doesn't change shape as you move around.

Step Four
Now that we have had some practice at creating the illusion that something is there it is time to introduce a storyline to our mime. My favourite is

"The Story of the Clumsy Burglar"
Two burglars break in to a house. They creep through the garden and push up the sash window. They carefully climb through but the clumsy one gets stuck. {Make sure you pick up the trailing leg over the window sill}. Once inside they search under and behind things.

The clumsy one nearly knocks over many things which are caught by the cool burglar. Eventually they find the safe and the cool one gets it open and loads the contents into a big box. They carry this heavy box between them back towards the window. The clumsy one stumbles and falls, there is a huge crash. They both run around panicking. They struggle through the window and suddenly stop. They raise their eyes as if they were looking at a very tall policeman. Up go their hands and they are arrested.

It will help you in your work if you talk about the layout of your imaginary room before you start so you both know where the window is and where the safe is, and so on. Exaggerate your movements to make it obvious what you are doing. DON'T SMILE.

When you are ready you can perform your work.

Top tip
I normally take a break from mime at this point and return to it later with the "Rollercoaster" unit and then the magician's magic box routine. It's important though to encourage the use of good simple mime in their other performance work.

Rollercoaster

This is a really good unit for getting groups buzzing and working together. The children will also practice a number of useful skills. If you enjoy this one you could turn it in to a main course by exploring the whole genre of disaster movies. Creating an earthquake through synchronised acting or a shaky camera for example.

Aims
To enhance motivation and develop the group dynamic.
To encourage observation.
To practice skills of synchronicity.
To develop the control involved in working in slow motion.

Resources
One chair each. Or nothing but a safe space if you want to go the whole hog.

Timescale
1 session for the basic plan. 2 or 3 more if you want to develop the plot and characters.

Method
Tell the story first.

"The worlds largest rollercoaster is about to open. There is going to be a gala event with pop stars and soap stars and even some footballers. There has been a competition and one of your group has won the lucky golden ticket so that you can go on the ride

It is the great day and everyone is there. One by one you get in to the carriage. When you are all seated you pull down the harness. It locks and you are about to go. There is a countdown. 5, 4, 3, 2, 1 and you are off. Hurtling up the first slope of many. You are flung to the left, to the right, down a huge drop. And so on. Finally you are brought to an abrupt stop which throws you forward and then back. You sigh with relief. You have survived!"

As a whole group practice this leading from the front encouraging everyone to take part. When they have it basically right give them a choice of different endings:

1. Near the end of the ride the carriage approaches a sharp bend. The track turns but the carriage doesn't and you all fly off. The last bit must be in slow motion and should not involve the chairs going over.

2. At the top of the highest rise the carriage grinds to a halt. You are all trapped! One of the passengers, probably a football hero, decides to go and get help. He climbs out and begins to walk down the track. Because the carriage is now lighter it slowly begins to move. He begins to run as it gathers speed. He gets further ahead and then he is caught up. Eventually he dives for the track and hides between the rails as the carriage shoots over him. {To achieve this he lies on his tummy and pushes himself backyards under the chairs, or just up stage of them.}

Now they can divide in to groups of 6 to 8 and work out their own rides to be performed when ready.

As a variation you can dispose of the chairs and have the children move in a double conga around the track, but only if you have space and feel that they will be safe.

To bring in more skills you could now incorporate your ride in to a disaster movie scenario with the usual stock characters. The ignored warnings, the accident and the fight for survival.

The whole of the above could also be adapted easily to fit around an Earthquake as the central piece of action. Video is useful if you do because camera shake can enhance the effect created by the children shaking, jumping and falling.

Everyone should survive.

Top tip
The basic movement work should be led by you but then they can diversify. The most effective bit is always the ride itself although older groups enjoy the characterisation aspects.

The Magicians Magic Box

This is one of my favourite routines but it is difficult so don't try it too early.

Aims
To further develop the children's physical mime skills
To encourage a sense of flourish and performance
To explore the comedy of mime
To provide a safe structure to encourage performance

Resources
None

Timescale
2 or 3 sessions depending on the group. With homework

Method
First tell them the routine whilst demonstrating yourself. You can use my script or take the bones of it and create your own version.

I would say:

There once was a Magician who thought he was very good. He had a glamorous assistant who wasn't really very interested and who often didn't pay enough attention.
Their act always finished with the magicians magic box routine.
In this routine the assistant pushes a wardrobe sized box on stage. {You pretend to do so}. The assistant, with great flourishes and a confident smile gets into the box and the door is closed {you do so}. Once out of the view of the audience the assistant stops acting and does something comic like picking their nose.
The magician now produces a number of swords, again with lots of flourish, which he now proceeds to push through the box. The assistant twists and turns with no show of interest in to an ever more contorted position. The final sword though, goes straight

through them and they are killed, silently but with lots of expression. They slump against the side of the {invisible}box.
The magician, not aware of the disaster, pulls out the swords one by one. As he does the dead assistant slumps more and more.
As the last sword comes out with blood on it the magician panics. He opens the door and the assistant falls forward. He is caught and pushed back in. the magician closes the door and holds it shut smiling nervously at the audience.
He then pushes the box off whilst smiling nervously. The assistant must shuffle sideways in the way described s to create the allusion that he or she are being pushed.
Neither the swords or the box actually exist. You might want to use a flowing robe so that you don't see the magicians feet.

Now you must practice the skills. First, the push.

In pairs, put your hands flat against those of your partner and pretend to push. Curve your back in and make your arms shake, but don't actually push. If you find this difficult practice against a wall and really push them take one step back and try to recreate the same effect.

When you are ready try the slump. This depends on you keeping your hips over your feet. Your knees go one way, your shoulders the other, and then you don't fall down. Again, you can try it with real supports and then remove them.

Now the walk. This hard and will need to be practiced for homework.

You start with toes together and heels apart.
Next you move your right foot till both feet are parallel, keeping the heel still.
Then you move the left foot, keeping the toes still, until your feet form a "V" shape.

Now move the right heel out to the right until your feet are parallel again.
Lastly you move the toes of your left foot to touch the toes of your right, forming a "V" facing backwards.

Repeat the movements in order and you will appear to glide sideways, especially if you are wearing a long kaftan or standing behind a table.

Once the skills have been mastered you can develop the comedy. The first fun is centre around the over the top flourishes. The next laugh comes when the assistant changes character once they are out of the view of the audience. Then the death and the comic slump. Then the reaction of the magician, and finally the glide off which is impressive when mastered.

Finish with performances and a debrief.

Top tip.
Many children will swing their hips rather then master the walk, it is though worth persevering because the sense of achievement when they get it right is immense.

Mix and Miss-match

This one has produced some of the funniest moments I've ever witnessed. You can use it as starter with experienced groups but it's most useful when enough rehearsal time is allowed to produce a polished result. Serious examples let the children explore a wide range of theatrical, dramatic and comic styles.

Aims
To introduce and explore a variety of theatrical styles and traditions in an entertaining and accessible way.
To develop the general skills involved in group improvisation and performance.
To stimulate creativity.
To practice and develop the discipline involved in performing comedy.

Resources
None but the space

Timescale
1 or 2 sessions then returned time and again

Method
I always start by exploring minimalism. Organise the children into groups in any way you want to and then ask them to choose a dramatic scenario, but be careful you don't tap in to their real life experiences. I usually go for things like, "My mum laid a new carpet, there was a bit of a lump, we flattened it and now we can't find the budgie", rather than dealing with tragedies in a family or serious illness.
Once they have decided on that they should explore performing it in an entirely neutral way. No facial expression, no vocal expression, hands on knees, knees together, sitting up and looking straight ahead.

When they get this right the contrast between the content and the style is hilarious.

Now you can have a discussion about the different conventions involved in a variety of theatrical and / or performance forms to create two lists. Then they can get to work performing one in the style of the other. I've listed some examples below to get you started. My favourite is a certain well known London based soap in the style of Grand Opera.

British Soap Opera	Grand Opera
American sit com	Country and Western
Crime Drama	Rural Soap, heavily accented
Children's TV Magazine	Minimalism or Neutrality
School based Drama	Melodrama
Saturday Morning Children's TV	Gothic Horror

Top tip
This works best, and is most useful in moving the children on, if they take it absolutely seriously. Also, when you have returned to this a few times, you will be able refer to the different styles and conventions in other settings.

Story Circles

Aims

To introduce and explore a variety of theatrical styles and traditions in an entertaining and accessible way.
To develop the general skills involved in group improvisation and performance.
To stimulate creativity.

Resources
None but the space

Timescale
1 or 2 sessions then returned to time and again.

Method
Sit the group in a circle, start three different plotlines yourself and send them off to left or right or bounce them across the way. Examples might be:

A group of foolish children decided to go exploring in the old mine.....
One morning, I woke to find a strange object in my garden.....
Mum just told me THAT cousin is coming to stay......

Each child in turn then has a chance to add a block to the story until you have a good solid beginning, then groups are formed, a plot chosen and off they go with their improvisations.

Top tip
You will need to restart a few times in the early days until they get the hang of what makes a story work in terms of plots and characters.

Creative Constraints

Aims
All of the usual plus
Promoting creative thinking by making the children fir to a tight framework.
Encouraging tight planning and group work.

Resources
None but the space

Timescale
1 or 2 lessons returned to on and off

Method
Use a board or flip chart to gather ideas. The constraint is that the plays must begin or end {and sometimes both} from a specific set of lines. The story, of course, must make sense of that. Examples might be:

"Some says, "I didn't mean it!" or
"I never expected THAT to happen!" or
"I'd have gotten away with it if it wasn't for those pesky kids!"

Top tip
Be strict. AS they develop you can add more constraints. Setting a strict performance time is a good one, usually between 3 and 5 minutes per improvisation.

Pantomime Plotlets
{Yes, that is a made-up word}

Aims
All the usual!

Resources
As you wish.

Timescale

2 to 3 lessons around Christmas.

Your task today is to take one of the plotlets below and use it as the beginning, middle or end of a play to be performed next week, with props, costume etc. if possible!

You also have to include at least ONE of the CONVENTIONS on the back!!

The Plotlets

1. Goldilocks {boy or girl} breaks in to a house in the forest where three "Bears" {human or otherwise} live. Why? Who is she or he? Who are they? What happens next..........

2. Cinderella. Her nice dad has married Bad. Step-mum is mean and the "sisters" are worse! They get to go to the Ball but not her. Until, the Fairy Godmother gets in on the act. All sorts of things get transformed and she gets to meet the "Prince". Happy ever after? You decide.......

3. Jack is a lazy lad. Mum tells him to sell the family cow {dog, hamster, granny} because they need some fast cash He gets conned into a bag full of beans BUT, one of them grows a magic beanstalk into a Cloud Kingdom! Star Wars meets Jack's Mum?

4. Ok, you get the idea. Snow White, Beauty and the Beast, Peter Pan, Aladdin….Can you do something special with these traditional stories?

Don't forget the CONVENTIONS below………………

And here they are!

You have to include at least one of these, but you should try to include as many as you can!

1. "The Juvenile" {young male] lead is actually a girl.

2. "The Dame" {older female comic character} is a boy.

3. There is a moment where the audience are asked to look out for the bad guys and shout "look behind you" to the good cast whenever the bad guys appear.

4. There should be a scene where the bad guy gets to say, "Oh no I didn't" to which the audience responds, "Oh yes you did" several times.

5. There should be a big bad character like a giant or a beast.

6. There should be an element of magic. {Maybe including a magic trick or transformation on stage}.

7. There has to be a happy ending for the main character, usually meaning disaster for the Bad Guys.

NB: You can give these traditional characters modern settings and re-work them, or create a pantomime story of your own in the same style!

Main Courses

There are additional skills involved in working on the same piece over long periods.

The units in this section can take up to 6 or 8 sessions to complete, with the possibility of more extension and result in polished performance pieces which are best done to an audience or to camera.

These are the real entrees of a successful drama menu and should be the main event in any effective drama course.

Don't just pick then off the shelf. Use the main ideas and use your own experience.

Most of all, enjoy.

The Experiment of Doctor Milo

The end result of this unit is usually a 15 to 20 minute play involving a cast of between 20 and 30 or so that can be performed to other classes or to parents or built up in to a full production. Changing the story and introducing new characters is perfectly acceptable. The original version began as class work from a group led by a young man called Joe Plass.

You can treat this as an improvisation using the student notes, or as a class play using the finished script, or even as a bit of both!

Aims

To give the students an improved understanding of the structure of plots and how they are developed

To develop an understanding of the creation and use of dialogue

To enable them to record their work as a script for the use of others

To provide an opportunity for the children to work on and improve their skills of characterisation

To guarantee a sense of ownership of the work

To allow talent to emerge and the children to find their comfort level

Or……..

To explore the problems and skills associated with the creation of character from a script

To look for the comic potential in a script and to explore ways of bringing it alive for the audience

To learn about the conventions of staging of melodramatic comedies.

IN ADDITION: You can use this to explore issues of parental responsibility, genetic cloning and adults views of children, to name but a few.

Resources
The full script if chosen
Help notes

Props / costumes provided by the children with your support
Whatever production aids or special effects you can manage

Timescale
At least 6 sessions but often as many as 10

Method
1. If you are going to use improvisation.

Tell them the story of the Experiment of Dr Milo. You can use the one below or personalise it to your own taste.

In a small town in a small county somewhere in _____ something strange was happening. One by one the children of the town were turning in to images of their own grandparents. None of them could remember how this happened and none could remember where they had been.

In the town there lived a boy called Martin. His parents were not getting on very well. They often argued and Martin spent a lot of time out. One morning his parents were cross with each other and ignoring him, eventually he stormed out. They didn't even notice.

Later, in the park, he was alone. Some nasty looking men leapt out and grabbed him and dragged him away. This was witnessed by his friends who had only just left him.

They rushed back to his house to tell his parents. At first his parents didn't believe them and the children left to try and rescue him them selves. When they were gone the parents reconsidered and called the police. The police decided to search for Martin and the parents decided to go with them.

They headed for the old laboratory from which mysterious sounds have been heard in recent weeks, but the children had beaten them to it. They had already sneaked past the guards and ended up lost inside the dark corridors.

Meanwhile Martin had been strapped to a bench in the Doctors laboratory ready to be subjected to Milos' experiment, the draining of the essence of his youth so that Milo could be young again!

Milos' daughter finds him, she seems to want to help but can't and Martin is left alone.

All of his friends had become separated and been captured, except Peter and Jill. They found Martin and were trying to release him, with the help of the daughter who had now changed her mind, but they were failing.

Milo and his henchmen rushed in and there was a dramatic confrontation between him and his daughter.

All seemed lost when the police and the parents burst in and, after a huge struggle, Milo was captured.

Enough elixir was found to restore all the children who had previously been taken and all was well.

And it still is……or is it?

Divide the class in to groups of about 10.

Give them the help notes and go through them briefly.

 Let them have a discussion about casting.

Move between the groups and help and encourage them as they develop the scenes.

Mix in performances of extracts and talk about the need to:
- Speak up and out
- Open the scene to the audience. Know where your audience is going to be
- Use the full space available to you
- Develop the action scenes for comic effect. E.g. The policemen could behave like escapees from an American cop movie

Also focus on the need to be supportive within the group of those who are less confident or less able.

Hot tip
This works best with older groups, years 8 or 9 {13 to 14 year olds}. Eventually they will be ready to perform. This is best to an invited audience because it gives it an edge.

2. If you are going to use the script.

In a circle read through the script taking volunteers and doing chunks yourself. Talk about the slap stick rolls of the guards and the policemen and experiment with styles like the ones mentioned above.

As a casting / development exercise, break them up in to groups of 4 or 5 and ask them to chose a section of the play to work on.
- Individuals can do Martin's monologue in the park
- Pairs can do the park scene with Peter and Jill
- Threes can do the first lab scene or the breakfast scene
- Fours can be the children in the park
- Larger groups can be the guards or do combinations of pieces

Next do some formal casting asking them to audition using the script. This is a real life experience and should be carefully handled. When you have cast it you can begin to rehearse.

Go through it once directing heavily. Then divide them up in to scenes.
- The guards can rehearse independently, as can the policemen
- The first and second scenes can be rehearsed simultaneously
- Only the last scene requires everyone

Keep everyone busy and use the performance of short extracts as master classes.

Learning lines is for homework or idle moments.

Perform to an invited audience when ready with as much production as you can manage!

Top tip
This approach works best with younger or less experienced groups. Years 6 and 7 really enjoy it.

<u>The Experiment of Doctor Milo.</u>
<u>Notes for the children</u>

<u>Scene 1</u>
In Dr Milos' laboratory a child is strapped to a table. The Doctor and his assistant are talking:
Dr   / No, No! It's no use. I've failed again! This child just doesn't have enough energy, I shall become old, as will all my clients. I'll never be able to sell my elixir.

Asst   / Oh Father. Can't you give it up? You're stealing the Youth of all these children. It's not worth it. How many more must you send back without their childhood.

Dr   / As many as it takes! I must succeed. I'm losing my hair. I have wrinkles. I'm overdrawn. I need more children! Guards!

{The guards enter marching and salute. This should be comical. Milo tells them to go and kidnap some more children.}

Scene 2
At Martins' house it is breakfast time. His parents are arguing and ignoring the fact that he is upset. In the end Martin shouts at them and runs out. They seem surprised.

Scene 3
In the Park the guards enter in disguise. Comically creeping about. Eventually they decide to lay a trap and hide.

Scene 4
Peter and Jill enter. He wants to ask her out and she wants him to but they are both embarrassed. He is about to finally ask when their friends enter. They talk about what to do because they are bored. The answer is always, "We did that yesterday".

Finally they all leave except Martin. He talks to himself {A Monologue} about his parents rows and how unhappy he is.} He is about to leave when the guards run out and grab him. There is a struggle but he is taken away. One of the girls sees this. She calls the others back and tells them. They decide to follow the guards and attempt a rescue.

Scene 5
Back at the house the children rush in. They tell Martins' parents but they think it is a joke. Dr Milo is a respected citizen. Frustrated, the children decide to return to Milos' laboratory them selves. After they leave the parents become worried and call the police. On the phone they agree to meet at Milos' to see what is going on.

Scene 6
In the lab martin is strapped down. Milo is about to switch on his machine laughing evilly. He says, "This time it will work and I will be rich and famous and young again etc."
He leaves to get something and martin pleads with the asst. to release him. She wants to but doesn't think she can betray her Father.

Scene 7
Outside the guards are on duty. The children trick them in some way. {E.g. "Look over there, someone's trying to steal your car"} The children get in to the building with the guards, eventually, going after them.

Scene 8
The children have separated and are looking for Martin. One by one they are captured. Peter and Jill get through and find Martin.
As they are trying to help, but failing, the asst. enters and decides to help. She shows them how to release him. They are about to escape when Milo bursts in.

"So, you would betray me! Now you also will be part of the experiment of Dr Milo"

"Father, No!"

As things are about to end badly for all the children the parents rush in with a Policeman. They try to capture Milo saying things like:

"Your evil reign is over"

"You'll never take me alive"

"Get him"

"Back, or I'll start the machine"

Etc.

Eventually the Policeman creeps up behind him and bashes him on the head. The children and the parents say:

"Hurray for the great British Bobby"

The lights fade over cheers.

Cast
Dr Milo
His daughter the assistant
First victim
Martin
Mum
Dad
Peter
Jill
Other children
Guards
Policeman

Hot tip
This is a great one to get the parents involved because the costumes are easy to achieve. I have included a fully developed script in case you are working with groups who would benefit from that.

The full script as we developed it. Change it at will!

Dr Milo's Experiment.

Scene 1

In the laboratory of Dr Milo. Milo is there with his daughter who is also his assistant. His latest victim is tied to the operating table.

Dr Milo / Now, finally, we can see if my experiment works! When I pull this leaver the child will become old and his essence will be stored in this bottle ready for my use and the use of my many very rich clients. I will be young and rich! Ha Ha!

Assistant / Oh Father, why do you have to be so evil? Why can't you be like other childrens fathers and do something more ordinary?

Dr Milo / Because I am the great Dr Milo and my work must go on. Think of it! A world in which people never get old!

Assistant / But only the rich people. What about the children whose childhood you are stealing?

Dr Milo / Pah. They don't matter. All they do with their childhood is play mindless games on computers and rush towards being grown up as fast as they can. I'm just helping them along a little.

Victim / Let me go you monster! I'm happy being a child and I don't want to grow up yet. It's just not fair.

Dr Milo / Oh be quite. You should have thought about that before you sneaked in to my garden to steal those apples. Now. Let us begin.

Milo and his assistant now start to twiddle with the knobs and leavers of his fiendish machine. There are sound effects. The child becomes old and wizened.

Dr Milo /   {*Holding up a small bottle*}. There! You see. It worked!

Assistant /   There's not very much of it.

Dr Milo /   You're right! I'm going to need a lot more than that. Hmmm. Guards!

The guards march in in a comic way. They stand to attention and salute.

Dr Milo /   Guards.

Guards /   Sir yes Sir.

Dr Milo /   Go in to the village and get me some more children. I need them for my experiment.

Guards /   Sir yes Sir

They exit equally comically

Dr Milo /   Now, let's see if we can make this machine more efficient. Release the child.

The Assistant does and then helps him off the stage.

Assistant /   You come with me and I'll make you a nice cup of tea.

Victim /   Oh thank you dear. You're a very kind young girl.

49

Everyone freezes as the lights fade to black.

Scene 2

In the kitchen of Martin's house. It is breakfast time and his parents are having their usual row. Martin is trying to say something but he can't get a word in edgeways.

Mum /	And if you didn't spend so much on your car we wouldn't be in this mess.

Dad /	Oh that's right, blame me and my car, just as usual. It's OK for you to go and buy yet another pair of shoes to add to all the other pairs of shoes you have in your new wardrobe but if I want to spend any money on the car, which, by the way, you are more than happy to be driven around in, then it's a problem.

Martin /	Mum, Dad.

Mum /	Be quiet Martin, we're talking.

Martin /	You're not talking you're arguing just like you always do and just like you always do you're ignoring me. Well I've had enough. I'm going to the park to see my friends because they understand me and they listen to me and I don't know when I'll be back as if you even cared.

Martin runs out. His parents stare after him.

Mum /	Do you think we've upset him?

They freeze as the lights fade to black.

Scene 3

In the park. The guards enter looking very suspicious. They might be wearing silly disguises. They creep around looking for children and / or for somewhere to hide. Occasionally they bump into each other as they walk backwards not looking where they are going.

Guard 1 / Ssshhh. We've got to be careful. If anyone sees us they'll run away and we won't be able to get any children for Dr. Milo.

Guard 2 / I really don't like it when Dr Milo gets cross. He's really scary.

Guard 3 / And he might decide to put us in his machine instead.

Guard 1 / Don't be silly. We're far too old for that.

Guard 2 / Far too old, far too old! But I'm only 12. *{Or whatever age you are}*

Guard 1 / Oh yes. Silly me.

Guard 3 / Let's hide over there, and then when those children appear we can grab one of them And Take them back to the laboratory. Quick, someone's coming.

The Guards all hide at the back of the stage as Peter and Jill enter. They could snigger with amusement at Peter's embarrassment. The children sit side by side but not too close.

Peter /   Jill………

Jill /   Yes Peter…..

Peter /   You know the other day when we were out with the others…..

Jill /   Yes Peter?

Peter /   And we got on really really well…….

Jill /   Did we Peter…….what's that noise? {*It is the guards sniggering*}

Peter /   Well I thought if we get on that well I thought that, well maybe you might………

Jill /   Might what?

Peter /   Might want to go ..{*The rest of this line is lost in the children's entrance which is very noisy*}.

Children / Hello Peter / hello Jill / what are you up to? / have you been waiting long? / what are we going to do now? / etc.

Martin /   Hello. Can we do something fun. I could do with being cheered up.

Peter /   Parents?

Jill /   Rowing?

Martin /   Yea. Same as ever. Never seems to stop. Just gets me down.

Child 1 /   {*If you have no extra children you can divide the lines between the main three characters*}. We could, climb that really big tree at the other end of the park.

Martin /   Did that yesterday.

Child 2 /   We could..... ride our bikes in the woods and build some jumps.

Martin /   Nah. No helmets.

Child 3 /   We could go and explore the old mansion on the hill and see if we can solve a mystery involving the caretaker.

Martin /   Nah. Too Scooby Do.

Child 1 /   Is there anything you're going to say yes to today?

Martin /   Don't think so.

Child 2 /   OK. Well then. We're going to the beach. If you want to you can join us later.

Martin /   All right then. I might. Thanks.

They all leave. Martin is left alone. He makes his big speech. This can be added to or cut down depending on the needs of the actor.

Martin /   Why don't they stop it? Why do they have to argue all the time? It didn't used to be like this. When did it start? I suppose it was when he got that new job. Away all the time. Always tired.
    It was nice to have all those things though. We couldn't afford them before, but then it all

53

started to go wrong. Now look at them, arguments for breakfast, dinner and tea. And they both look so tired.

I want to tell them. I want to say sell the car, get rid of my play station, go back to how it used to be. I don't care about the big new house and nor should you.

But they won't listen. I'm just a kid, so what do I know? I hate all this…

At this point the guards run in. There is a struggle, which could be partly in slow motion, and Martin is dragged off. Jill and Peter re-enter.

Jill and Peter / Did you see that. Somebody has grabbed Martin. This is terrible. Let's tell his parents. They'll know what to do!

They exit.

Scene 4

In the kitchen of Martin's house. His parents are still arguing.

Both /   AND another thing!

Peter /   Mr and Mrs Phillips! You never guess what's happened!

Mum /   Martin has been kidnapped.

Jill /   Yes! How did you know.

Dad /   Oh it's not the first time. Whenever we have a bit of a disagreement there's something. Tree house on

	fire, trouble at school, abducted by space aliens. So staging his own kidnap is quite tame really.
Peter /	But he didn't. There were guards. Really big ones.
Jill /	And they grabbed him and there was a fight and he struggled but they still took him.
Peter and Jill /	It was horrible.
Mum /	Yes, yes. Would you like some milk?
Peter /	Oh you're hopeless. We'll go and rescue him ourselves!

They exit in a hurry. Mum and Dad look at each other looking confused.

Dad /	Do you think it might be for real this time?
Mum /	I don't know. I suppose we could just check with the police to see if there is a gang of suspicious people in the area.
Dad /	OK. You call the Police and I'll get the wellies.
Mum /	Right. {*She dials*}. Hallo, is that the police? I'd like to report a missing child...... How Many?.......Oh Daddy......It's true......They said to meet them at the laboratory of Dr Milo!

They freeze as the lights fade to black

Scene 5

Back in the laboratory of Dr Milo, Martin is strapped to the table as the Dr and his assistant adjust the machine.

Dr Milo / Now I will succeed. This one is full of youthful energy. With him I can make enough elixir to satisfy all my customers as well as myself. Ha Hah!

Assistant / It's not fair and you know it. You had your childhood leave the children to enjoy theirs.

Dr Milo / Silence! You know better than to argue with me in front of the victims, or even at all! This machine is big enough for two if you have a problem with this experiment!

Martin / Let me go Milo. You won't get away with this! My friends know where I am and they will come and rescue me.

Dr Milo / Pah! A bunch of hapless children against my guards, I really don't think so…….. On the other hand……I'd better go and check the alarms. Keep an eye on him but don't start the machine till I get back. I want to see this one myself!

Milo leaves

Martin / You don't agree with him….do you.

Assistant / Be quiet. You're not meant to talk to me. The Doctor wouldn't like it.

Martin / Look. If you don't agree with him why not help me and then we can escape together. You can come

	back with me. We'll get the Police and stop Milo. It is possible. Believe me. You know you want to.
Assistant /	You don't understand. Milo took me in when there was no one else to look after me. I know what he's doing is wrong but I owe him so much.
Martin /	You owe more to yourself. Anyway, he's ill, he has to be if he thinks this is right. Let me go and we can get help for him.
Assistant /	Help? Really? Well…. Perhaps….

The Assistant begins to undo one of the straps when Milo walks in

Dr Milo /	So! This is how you reward my kindness. Betrayal at the first chance you get! Now you also will become part of the Experiment of Dr Milo!

Milo pushes the Assistant in to the machine and straps her in. He is laughing madly as the lights fade to black.

Scene 6

At the Police station the policemen are having a quiet day. They enter like the LAPD.

Policeman 1 /	{after he has got his breathe back}. Doesn't anything ever happen in this town? The most exciting thing that's happened in the last three months in this town was Mrs. O'Connell's cat getting trapped in her willow tree, and that's only 6 feet tall.
Policeman 2 /	Oh I don't know. I gave out lots of parking fines yesterday. I enjoyed that.
Policeman 1 /	It's not like this in the movies. I only joined up for the fast cars and the excitement and look what's

happened. My patrol car is a mini metro and my main pastime is rescuing moggies from weeping willows.

At this point the children burst in. They are breathless and very excited.

Children /	Officers, officers. You've got to help us. It's Dr Milo, he's kidnapped Martin and we think it's part of an evil international conspiracy!

Policeman 1 /	Dr Milo? An evil international conspiracy. Get away. Dr Milo is a respected local business man. I mean, we both belong to the same club. I can't believe he'd be a part of an international conspiracy, or even a local conspiracy for that matter.

Children /	But he is! You've got to believe us. Just because we're children doesn't always mean we don't know what we're talking about. HELP US!

Policeman 2 /	Well Chief. It might be worth investigating. At least it will get us out of the station. Bit of a change.

Policeman 1 /	I don't know. Dr Milo might get upset if we march in there and accuse him of being part of an international conspiracy. I mean, it's not nice.

Children /	Oh for goodness sake. We haven't got time to listen to this. You adults are all the same. Talk, talk, talk. We'll just have to rescue him ourselves. Come on kids. To Milo's laboratory.

They rush off leaving the policemen open mouthed.

58

Policeman 1 / Well, that was a bit of a turn up. You don't think they'll do anything silly do you?

Policeman 2 / I don't know. They were very excited though. Perhaps we should pop along to Dr Milo's laboratory, just in case anything goes wrong. We wouldn't want anything to go wrong now, would we.

Policeman 1 / Perhaps you're right. And it will be more exciting than watching the kettle boil ready to make yet another cup of English tea. Let's get ready.

There could now be an action sequence when the police put on dark glasses and exit in dramatic fashion.

Scene 7

Outside the Laboratory of Dr Milo. The Guards are guarding, badly

Guard 1 / *{Reading from a magazine}*. It says here, that the solar system is hurtling through space at more then 600,000 miles an hour and that the Earth goes round the Sun at more then 60,000 miles an hour which means that we are 6,000,000 miles away from where we **were** when we went to bed yesterday.

Guard 2 / And people say we don't travel enough, huh.

Guard 3 / Stop it. You're making me feel dizzy. I feel like I need to hold on.

Guard 2 / Let's do something.

Guard 3 /   I suppose we could do some marching about, after all we are meant to be Guards.

The Guards now get in line and perform a comedy marching routine in which they drop everything and regularly bounce off each other. After a while Dr Milo enters.

Guard 1 /   Guards! Attention!

They sort of manage it and Dr Milo is quiet impressed.

Dr Milo /   Very good guards, one of your better efforts. Now listen. I have reason to believe that a group of pesky children may try and sneak in to my laboratory. Your mission, should you choose to accept it, is to stop them. Is that clear.

Guards /   Yes Dr Sir, Yes Sir.

Dr Milo /   And try not to look too conspicuous. We don't want to attract to much attention, Put on these disguises.

The Guards put on whatever comes to hand

Dr Milo /   Good, that's much better. Right, you get back to your guarding and I'll get back to my experiment.

Dr Milo exits and the Guards stand about looking inconspicuous. The children sneak in and hide in the corner.

Child 1 /   Ssshhh. Look, this must be the place. There are guards.

Child 2 /   How do you know they are guards? They don't look like guards.

Child 3 /	Look at their boots silly. Guards are a bit like policemen, they always wear big boots.
Child 2 /	Oh, I see, I think.
Child 1 /	We'll have to think of a way to get past them.
Child 2 /	We could pretend we had an appointment with the Doctor because we aren't very well.
Child 3 /	Nah, too easy.
Child 1 /	We could get them to join in a game of hide and seek and when it's their turn to hide we can just walk in.
Child 2 /	Brilliant! Let's do it.

The children come out looking deliberately sweet and innocent.

Child 3 /	Oh dear. It's such a long time till dinner and we've nothing to do.
Child 1 /	I suppose we could play a game…….like hide and seek.
Child 2 /	Nah, you can't play hide and seek with three people. You need loads more than that.
Child 3 /	I wonder if there is anybody who might be able to help us?
Child 1 /	I really don't know.

Guard 1 / We could play, if you like. {Aside} The Dr said to look incospi, inconspi, not to get noticed. Playing with a bunch of kids is just the thing.

Child 2 / Oh thank you. Now hide and seek will be loads of fun. Tell you what, you go and hide first and I'll come seeking for you.

Guard 2 / OK. Come on then.

The other children pretend to hide as the Guards actually do. Child 1 counts to 10 and then beckons the others to follow. They creep in to the entrance to the laboratory. Eventually the Guards look up.

Guard 3 / Where have they gone?

Guard 2 / You don't think they went in to the laboratory do you?

Guard 1 / Rats! They must have been the children the Doctor warned us about! Quick! We have to catch them before the Doctor finds out.

The Guards also rush in to the Laboratory. As they disappear Mum and Dad enter with the Police who are still jumping about like action movie heroes.

Mum and Dad / It must be this way. Hurry, there's no time to waste.

Policeman 1 / Come on lads. We've got to get to those kids before they get to the Doctor whichever way you look at it.

They also rush in to the Laboratory ready for the final scene

Scene 8

This starts with the end of scene 5

Dr Milo /   So! This is how you reward my kindness. Betrayal at the first chance you get! Now you also will become part of the Experiment of Dr Milo!

Milo pushes the Assistant in to the machine and straps her in. He is laughing madly as he prepares to start up the machine

Martin /   Don't do it Dr! It's wrong and you know it. I need my childhood and so does he / she. Let us go!

Dr Milo /   Never! I've gone too far to stop now. Think of all the old people who will thank me. Each of you will restore the youth of 10 of them.

Assistant /   You're ill Father, let me help you. It's not too late.

Dr Milo /   Pah! Enough of this. Prepare to become part of the experiment of Dr Milo!

As the machine starts to warm up the guards enter with most of the children. They have captured them.

Guard 1 /   Look Dr. We have found some more.

Children /   Let us go!

Guard 2 /   Only if you say pretty please.

Children /   No!

Dr Milo / Into the machine with them! At this rate we'll have enough elixir to open shop in Eastbourne!

The guards tie the struggling children in to the machine

Dr Milo / Now, where was I? Oh yes, the final countdown.

At this point Peter and Jill rush in

Peter and Jill / Stop! They are our friends

Dr Milo / Pesky kids! You can't find any for months and then they turn up by the dozen. In to the machine with them.

As the guards reach for them the scene goes in to slow motion as Peter reaches out to try and turn off the machine. He fails and they are both grabbed and installed

Dr Milo / Now, finally…..

The Policemen and Mum and Dad enter at the same time from different sides of the stage

Policemen / Hold it right there Milo. We see you now for what you are. Let the children go!

Dr Milo / Oh for goodness sake. Guards, get them.

The guards and the policemen now have a brief fight and the guards are overpowered. Meanwhile Dr Milo has tired to creep out but Mum has got him in an arm lock

Dad / Well done mum. I knew you could do it.

Dr Milo /   Unhand me woman. You don't know who you're dealing with!

Mum /   Yes we do and we don't care!

Children /   Hooray for Martin's Mum

All /   *{Except the Policemen}* And hooray for the Great British Bobby!

Dr Milo /   Darn it. I'd have got away with it if it wasn't for them pesky kids.

Black out

The End…..or is it.

Time Capsule

This idea is adapted from the biscuit tin full of newspapers so favoured by a certain children's TV magazine programme.

Aims
To encourage the children to take a good look at the world in which they live. The unit operates at different levels depending on the choice of materials so you can tailor it to the needs of your groups. The children will also be encouraged to explore the problems associated with performing different sorts of drama. Many of them will produce narrative plays, some will use parody, others documentary styles.
All will need to come to terms with the needs of the camera.

Resources
A video camera

Timescale
Flexible. Between 4 and 8 sessions

Method
Explain to the children the concept of a time capsule. Bring in the following points as appropriate:-
- Things which are ordinary to them might be unusual to people in the future. For example their children might only go to school for lessons which need other people, if at all. They might mostly be taught by a computer that they can speak to and which will answer.
- Family life could be very different. Mum, Dad and siblings in one house is only one way of organising bringing up children. Why not have 16 parents and all live in huge houses.
- Work will have changed, it's changing now. Car factories that used to employ 7000 men are now run by half a dozen.

- To us space travel is an adventure or an impossible dream. Will it be to them?
- What will they find attractive? What will they think of fashion today, of our music, of the things we like to buy, and especially our sense of humour.
- Will they think well of us and the care we have or haven't taken of their Planet.

When the discussion naturally ends explain that you are going to make a time capsule tape of your work and seal it in foil and put in a box and bury it for future generations to find. When they do those who appear in the tape will be world famous.
They will need to make up performance pieces to be filmed. They might do one long one or many short pieces.
Once in a while all work will be stopped whilst the most recent batch of pieces are filmed.
When the tape is full. Bury it.

Give them advice about how to proceed using the following guidance:-
- Smaller groups are easier to work in than larger groups.
- Fashion shows or short pieces about modern music are really straight forward.
- The next simplest response is to make up plays which show different aspects of life at school. Lessons, teachers, problems, highlights.
- Next, work. For example the monotony of working on a production line.
- Next, home life. It could be funny or serious, just show them some experiences of family life, good and bad.
- Next, entertainment. How do we amuse ourselves. Samples of TV programmes, Film reviews like film 2004/5/6/7. Their own versions of comedy shows or sketches.
- Performances about how they see the future are always fun, probably more so for anyone in the future who sees the tape. Automated houses, robots that look like people

and then go wrong. Or a future in which the world has been invaded by aliens, who might be invisible. The possibilities are endless.
- For children who want more of a challenge. A programme about issues, or an issue. Examples might be Homelessness in one of the world's richest countries. The first world / third world divide. Pollution, the ozone layer, the destruction of the rain forests, the slaughter of the whales, or anything else over which they have real concerns and about which they can do some genuine research. These programmes could include "Interviews", live action extracts, pre recorded footage and allsorts.

As they work move from group to group and problem solve. Be ready to film at any point after the end of the 2nd session.

Top tip
This one has worked best for me with year 6 groups, but you could start it when a group is young and keep taping, on and off, until the last member of the group leaves.
This would then become not just an archive of our times, but also of their development.

The Seven Stories

There are meant to be Seven plots which cover the whole of human creativity in any medium. I'm not sure I believe this but I've been trying for years, and so have endless classes of students, to find one that doesn't. In the context of plays it depends on which character or group of characters you focus on. The "Cinderella" plot is only that from the viewpoint of Cinderella, the Ugly Sisters story is very different.

Whatever your view of all this, this idea provides a great way to explore the mechanisms of story telling and the students find it very stimulating.

Aims
The primary aim is to encourage the students to think about plots and stories and how they work. Whilst they work through this they will explore how to create tension and conventions about staging. There will also be many opportunities to practice their skills of characterisation and also those skills associated with group work over prolonged periods.

Resources
Display of 7 story lines

Timescale
Up to 6 to 12 sessions, possibly interspersed with other units.

Method
Explain to the children that there are, in theory, only seven story lines and that all the books that they have read or films that they have seen fit into one of these, although some are a combination and which storyline applies depends on which characters point of view you are telling the story from. Make sure there is a large visual display of the seven stories as described below. Only go through them as each storyline is initiated. 4, 6 and 7 are the most difficult. I usually focus on 1 to 4 and then just tell the rest.

When each story has been explained give them a session to work out their performances and then watch them in the second. Some groups will take longer.

You may decide to shorten the unit by allocating a storyline to each group so you can have 4 or 5 going at once, and then debrief. You could keep this secret and ask the other groups to identify which storyline each play was based on.

You may choose to ignore the Hollywood contribution on the grounds that there is never any real resolution.

These are the seven stories.

1. CINDERELLA. A story of a person whose life is based on good and bad luck. Or, a person who finds their destiny after suffering.
2. ACHILLES. The story of someone successful who is brought down by a single flaw or weakness.
3. CIRCE. The story of the spider and the fly on which most horror stories are based.
4. ORPHEUS. Or the gift that is taken away. Often a story of illness or injury, sometimes in love and sometimes in war.
5. ROMEO AND JULIET. Love or friendship across the divides of a community. Often based on gangs or race or class prejudice.
6. TRISTAN. The eternal triangle. A three-way relationship often involving career, money, power, fast cars or just a lover or third close friend.
7. FAUST. The story of the promise that must be kept. Usually when the person hadn't realised the consequences or thought that they could avoid them.

Hollywood claim an eighth story.

8. THE STORY OF THE INDOMITABLE HERO. That is somebody who can never be defeated regardless of the odds, like Indiana Jones or James Bond.

Group sizes should be the usual 4 to 6 and your approach should be age related. All students will cope with "Cinderella"; most would struggle with "Faust".

As they are creating your role is that of the facilitator, moving from group to group as needs arise.

Top tips
Young groups like number 1. Both years thrive on number 3. Boys tend to like number 8.
A thirty minute scripted version of number 5 which has a proven record of success with year 6 is available on Amazon.
Year 6 deal well with the rest and this unit can provide a good stimulus for examination groups.
It would be interesting to produce some plot digests of plays that they are going to come across further up the school in English and to see if they can correctly identify which group it belongs to.
This activity also lends itself to Hot seating {where an actor is interviewed in character} since the characterisations can be quite intense in the more serious stories.

Radio Station

This one is a firm favourite with children who want to perform but find it very hard. It's also a good one for calming down an "over excited" group because it's static and relatively quiet.

Aims
Apart from the above…..
To develop their awareness of the importance of timing and planning
To give shy children the opportunity to gain confidence
To develop the use of voice to communicate meaning and action
To allow for a sharing of music and culture
To encourage children to listen to more varied radio!

Resources
A tape recorder with a microphone
Possible various sound effects creators {dried peas etc}
A screen big enough to shield the group from view
Sound effect CD's and a player, if you have them

Timescale
Introducing, planning and rehearsal should take 4 sessions, recording and performing, a further 2

Method
Play the group some recorded samples of different radio stations. Try to include as many different programmes and styles as possible. Set them the task of producing 5 minutes of air time with samples only of a variety of programmes. These should include a soap, an interview, news and weather, maybe a quiz in the form of a competition, a play with sound effects, some music but intros only, and their own ideas.
In groups they should carefully plan their work, ideally scripting everything unless this would become a barrier to learning.
They should bring in their own home made sound effects equipment, or at least organise it.

Exploring the World of Dreams.

The possibilities of dreams are endless. This work often ends in mime or movement, dance or multi media pieces. Some of the best work we have ever done has resulted from this unit.

Aims

To tap in to one of the most stimulating and personal areas of human existence as a stimulus for a drama presentation which explores unusual forms, ultimately blending drama with dance and abstract expression.

As part of this to introduce the student to less obvious dramatic conventions, to theatre in a more avant guard and unusual form.
To encourage sharing in a supportive atmosphere.
Where possible, to explore how technical support can enhance the performance of created pieces.

Resources

You can achieve great results with a spacious room and nothing else. You might also use percussion, rain sticks, recorders, CD sound tracks, coloured light, strobe, smoke, gauze, reflection, video, live sound recording with echo and / or distortion and anything else you or they can think of and provide.

Timescale

Anything from 6 sessions upwards

Method

In a conducive atmosphere with the children close and quiet, introduce the topic of "Dreams". Emphasise that if their dreams are too personal or private they should not share. Tell some stories of dreams. These may be your own, those of friends or just famous examples.

Have a sharing session in which the children tell the group of some of their dreams. Tease out elements which are common to the dreams of many people. These might include:-
- Flying

When they are able to run the show without faltering they can take it in turns to record behind the screen. This is the performance. The tape is for your records and the debrief, so that they can hear how well they have done.

Top tips
It's often funny to plan in errors, the microphone that is left on, or open, the wrong sound effects etc. With big groups you will need to shorten the air time or have them work in larger groups.
With the right class they could all work on their own contribution to one broadcast, with one group in charge of melodrama, another music and a third the news etc.
Some groups will want to develop the idea and produce some programming for a TV channel, in which case you could take a year!

- Weightlessness
- Repetition
- Trying to scream or speak but no sound coming out
- Trying to move forward and feeling too heavy to get anywhere
- Familiar people behaving out of character
- Things that have happened to you that day emerging jumbled up
- Being high up and feeling precarious
- Impossible creatures
- Suddenly being somewhere else for no apparent reason
- Other things which emerge from the contributions of the children

Divide them into groups of 6 or so, more or less if you recognise a need, and give them time, in small groups, to share and begin to decide on the content of their groups dream presentation.

When you judge the time to be right stop them and talk about how they might present and develop their work. You could include:-
- Repetition and echo
- Mime
- Slow motion
- Dance or rhythmic movement
- The use of sound effects
- The use of light changes
- Thought tracking {where an offstage actor speaks the thoughts of an on stage character who's face and actions reflect the internal dialogue}
- Any others that you feel will be useful

Let them work on and intervene as necessary moving towards a final performance.
Video the results and debrief, or just debrief.

Top tip
It's best to use this piece before the students reach that awkward age, or for advanced work with groups who are confident in them selves and their colleagues.

Silent Movie

Silent Movies are becoming a lost art form. For that reason alone this is a valuable piece of work.

Aims

To encourage the students to explore physical acting by removing speech from the performance.

To give them an understanding of how acting to camera works differently.

To acquaint them with a classic form of entertainment.

To practice all the usual skills involved in developing group work over a long period of time.

To further develop their understanding of how stories are constructed and communicated through choice of scenes.

Resources

This depends on how complex you can or want to be. You will need a video camera and sufficient tapes. A4 plain paper and large pens are also essential. If you went the whole way you might want costumes, sugar glass bottles, cut outs of trains and so on. But you only need the camera and the paper.

Timescale

Anything from 6 sessions to 12 or more

Method

You could begin by showing the group some extracts from classic silent movies if you can do so without infringing copyright. There are many websites that are really informative, just type in "Silent Movies". Otherwise you can tell them all about it. The following is something like the version they get from me.

"When films were first made they could record the pictures but not the sound. Well, they could record the sound but they couldn't get it to match up with the pictures so they couldn't use it. Instead they

used caption cards with the words written on them and a musician in the cinema who would play the music live to match the scene on the screen. So for a chase you would get, {they will tell you}, Most movies fitted in to one of the following groups: -
- Horror films like "Frankenstein".
- Westerns where the good guys wore white hats and the bad guys didn't.
- Comedies like the ones with Charlie Chaplin
- And Melodramas where the soppy girl has to be rescued by the hero from the evil landlord who has tied her to the railway track.

If you want to you can join some of these up or try and invent a new story, but, it must be silent. And remember, you are going to film this not perform it as a play so you can stop and move the camera to make it look better, or to change the scene. You must though do the scenes in the right order and you only get one go.

In between scenes you will need caption cards that say things like, "Meanwhile, on the far side of town" or "Gasp". Do not have more than six of these because each one involves stopping the camera to film the card in close up. You can have extra title and credits pages.

When I have answered any questions you are to get in to groups of around 5 or 6, without leaving anyone out, and sit down to discuss and decide which sort of film you want to make. Call me over to OK it when you are ready. Then you can cast your selves and begin to plan your scenes.

When you have done that you can get up and begin to rehearse.

Now go."

When they are working you will be free to move around problem solving and contributing ideas. The films will evolve over a number of sessions and usually end up at about 5 minutes long. Horrors and Melodramas are the most popular choices.

The final session can be a premier and then review.

Top tips
Resist the requests from the children to be allowed to operate the camera.
When you are filming make sure the actors fill the frame and don't let them do retakes unless you intend to edit and have the facilities to do so.
In the later stages of rehearsal let each group perform in the actual space and have a clearly marked point which is the camera so that they can get used to focusing their work in that direction.

Jason and the Argonauts

Great tales provide great opportunities, and this one has it all. Heroes and villains, monsters, romance, adventure, betrayal and if you want to, lots of gore.

I've included some work attached to this project that you could use to extend the work into literacy and history at least, which I hope you find useful. You could easily extend it into a huge multidisciplinary project if that was your need. Music and dance often naturally arise and phse issues could easily be raised. A full scheme of work and templates for the worksheets are available on the CD.

Aims

So far as drama is concerned

To further explore and develop the skills involved in complex story telling. These involve:
- The selection of material and plot points
- The development of character
- An awareness of pace and structure
- An awareness of the needs of the Audience
- Applying practical limitations to their work whilst still be adventurous

Resources

From nothing but a space to everything you need for a fully staged show.

I usually get by with a few plastic swords, some simple costume and some percussion instruments, although I must confess to a smoke machine.

Timescale

At least 6 sessions, and often a whole terms work.

Method
In discussion let them tell you some legends. You might heighten there interest by telling them about the archaeological finds that support the truth of some elements of these tales. For example:
- During the excavation of the palace of Knossos on Crete they found a labyrinth
- We know that the Island of Santorini was all but destroyed by a cataclysmic volcanic eruption between 1600BC and 1400BC. Many believe that the devastation this caused to Minoan Crete was the origin of the legend of Atlantis
- The discovery of the site of Troy in western Turkey by Schliemann
- And, most interestingly, villagers in the mountains of Northern Turkey get the gold out of rivers by weighting fleeces down at the bottom of streams so that the gold is caught in the wool!

When the time is right you can tell them the story of Jason and the Argonauts. You might want to use my notes, or research your own version. Worksheets linked to this, which support literacy, are available as free downloads from the website.

My notes
The Story of the Golden Fleece.
Jason was the rightful King of Iolcus in ancient Greece. His Father died when he was young so his uncle ruled for him. His name was Pelias.

Pelias sent Jason away to be educated by a wise Centaur called Chiron. A centaur was a wise creature with the body of a horse and the torso, head and arms of a man.

When Jason had grown up he went back to claim his throne.

Pelias didn't like this idea but he was afraid of Jason because he arrived wearing only one shoe {He'd lost the other one crossing a stream on the way to the Palace} and Pelias had been warned by an Oracle, or fortune teller, that a man with one shoe would cause his death.

He got Jason to agree that he had to go on a quest to prove that he was worthy of being a King before Pelias handed over power.

The quest was to be the search for the Golden Fleece.

Jason gathered together a band of Heroes to help him. This band included
AMPHION   THE DIOSCURI PELEUS   MELEAGER
     ORPHEUS   THESEUS   and   HERCULES
All of whom had special skills.

They sailed on the Argo, a ship of fifty oars, and had many adventures.

These included dealing with THE HARPIES, THE SIRENS, A RACE OF GIANTS and THE CLASHING ROCKS. There could be others, e.g. MEDUSA, the snake haired woman whose gaze could turn men to stone.

Eventually they reached the kingdom where the fleece was kept, which was ruled by King Aeetes.

Aeetes set Jason some tasks to complete before he could have the fleece.

These involved harnessing two wild bulls with hooves of bronze and breathe of fire and then ploughing a field and sowing some dragon teeth.

Jason succeeded but when he sowed the seeds skeleton warriors sprang from the ground and fought him. They lost.

Jason was able to do this because Medea, daughter of Aeetes, had fallen in love with him. She was a beautiful sorceress and she used her magic to help him.

Next Aeetes tried to get Jason killed by sending him off to get the fleece without telling him about the Seven headed Hydra that guarded it. Again Medea saved him by drugging the beast.

They now fled with Aeetes in hot pursuit. To slow him down Medea killed her own brother and left him in the road.

When they got back to Iolcus, Pelias was not happy and refused to give up power. Medea arranged his death by tricking his own daughters in to killing him. Pelias was very ill and the daughters came to her for help. She showed them her skills by sacrificing a sheep and then bringing it back to life. She told them that she could do the same for Pelias so they killed him, but then she refused! But the people were unhappy and both she and Jason had to flee.

At first they lived happily but them Jason fell in love with somebody else.
Medea was furious and cast a spell that killed Creusa, Jasons bride, on their wedding day. Medea pretended to accept her and gave her a fabulous dress for her wedding present, but when she got to the alter it burst in to flames.

Medea went back to her father who had now forgiven her. Jason grew old and people forgot about him. One day he was resting under the bow of the Argo, which was out of the water, when the ship fell on him and he was killed.

Next discuss the key points of the story. I.e. Which scenes must you show and which might scenes you show?

83

Now the characters. There must be a Jason, but if you have lots of budding stars why not have a Jason costume which they take it in turns to wear. Characters you can not cast can be covered by narration.
Finally, before groups are formed {normally 6 to 8}, explain to them that legends evolve and that if they have new ideas, or want to import characters or stories from other legends, that's fine. After all, this one already involves Hercules, Theseus and Orpheus so why not a few more. They should though be in the right period and style, no heroic turtles or human bats.

Now let them go and provide help where needed. You might want to film the final outcomes

Top tips
The best results I've had with this project have been with year 6, although 7's and 8's have also produced excellent work.
As it develops and you discuss with them the problems they tend to come up with great solutions, often involving simple music and rhythm or fabulous costumes.
You could also look for appropriate comedy, the hydra arguing with itself never fails.
As to the gore, I tend to avoid the slaughter of the children but allow the deaths of Pelias and Creusa and that seems to work.

Desserts

Just one dessert, but one so popular that you never get tired of trying it again.

Oscars

This is a celebration of the childrens' success. It needs no other aims or justification.

Every once in a while announce an Oscars Awards Ceremony to be imminent.

The children can work in groups of their own choosing to create work of their own devising to be performed at the time of your choice to the academy, {yourself and a colleague, or sometimes parents}.

Oscars will be awarded in categories chosen by you. There will be enough of them to make sure that everyone wins something.

Here are some sample categories that you might want to base your ceremony around

Best Actor {Boy or Girl}
Best Comedy Performance
Best Comedy Moment
Most Dramatic Moment
Best Opening
Best Ending
Best use of Props
Best use of Space
Most Co-operative group
Best Group Leader
Best Story

Best Costume
Most Amusing Costume
Best use of Sound {Usually original music played live}
Loudest Group
Most Sensible Group
Best Newcomer in a Leading Role
Best Newcomer
Most Annoying Student!

In my sessions Oscars consist of certain small person like sweets, but you can also use certificates or other prized prizes of their choice or your own.

A few thoughts on assessment and evaluation
My criteria for a successful lesson are:
Did the children arrive early and smiling?
Did they just get on with a game without prompting?
Did they involve everyone as a matter of course?
Were they fully on task all the way through?
Did they want to stay even if break was happening elsewhere?

And as time goes by:
Were they prepared to take on more complex challenges?
Were they willing and able to work in varied groups, even with people they don't like?

Which involves:

Were they able to leave their arguments at the door because good drama lessons were more important?
Is everyone in the group comfortable performing?

Can do statements
Drama. Indicators of success!

Introduction	I can enter sensibly and quickly sit quietly. **I can take a positive part in the warm up.** I can listen to, understand and follow instructions.
Planning	I can work effectively in small groups. I can stay in my own groups' rehearsal space. **I can listen, discuss and decide without arguing or over reacting.** I can show respect to everyone. **I can work without bringing personal issues in to the main lesson.**
Performance	I can plan a performance piece with a good ending. **I can be aware of the audience needs and**

	make sure they understand. I can perform with confidence in class. **I can use basic mime skills to create a sense of where I am and what I am doing.** I can create character by behaving differently and using voice. **I can react positively to feedback to move my work forward.**
Audience	I can settle quickly. **I can show respect by paying proper attention and not calling out.** I can show appreciation by clapping at the right time. **I am able to comment positively on my own work and the work of others.**

And finally

When you announce a school production that is not compulsory, how many children turn up to audition!

And finally, finally

You will find many plays written by Gareth Jones available on Amazon. The series is called, "New Comedies for all Stages" and they are suitable for KS2. The USP? Buy a cast set and there are no royalties!

Printed in Poland
by Amazon Fulfillment
Poland Sp. z o.o., Wrocław